▲▲▲▲▲▲▲▲▲▲▲▲▲▲▲▲▲▲▲▲▲▲▲▲▲▲▲▲▲▲▲▲▲

# L I F E W A Y S

The Haida

# R A Y M O N D   B I A L

▼▼▼▼▼▼▼▼▼▼▼▼▼▼▼▼▼▼▼▼▼▼▼▼▼▼▼▼▼▼▼▼▼

**BENCHMARK BOOKS**

MARSHALL CAVENDISH
NEW YORK

SERIES CONSULTANT: JOHN BIERHORST

ACKNOWLEDGMENTS

The Haida was published through the assistance of many people and organizations, who have devoted themselves to preserving the arts and traditions of the Haida. I am especially grateful to Jennifer Webb and the Museum of Anthropology at the University of British Columbia. I would like to express my appreciation to Arthur Olivas of the Museum of New Mexico for his gracious help in locating several photographs. I would also like to thank the British Columbia Archives, the Royal British Columbia Museum, the National Archives, the Library of Congress, and the Philbrook Museum of Art for providing a number of fine illustrations for this book.

I would like to thank Kate Nunn and Doug Sanders for their hard work in editing and generally bringing all the various parts of this book together. I am again very much indebted to John Bierhorst for his thorough review of the manuscript and many insightful suggestions. Once again, I reserve my deepest appreciation to my wife, Linda, and my children Anna, Sarah, and Luke for their wonderful support.

Benchmarks Books
Marshall Cavendish Corporation
99 White Plains Road, Tarrytown, New York 10591-9001
Text copyright © 2001 by Raymond Bial
Map copyright © 2001 by the Marshall Cavendish Corporation
Map by Rodica Prato

Library of Congress Cataloging-in-Publication Data
Bial, Raymond.
The Haida / Raymond Bial.
cm. — (Lifeways)
Includes bibliographical references and index.
Summary: Discusses the history, culture, social structure, beliefs, and customs of the Haida people.
ISBN 0-7614-0937-8
1.Haida Indians—History—Juvenile literature. 2. Haida Indians—Social life and customs— Juvenile literature. [1. Haida Indians. 2. Indians of North America—British Columbia. 3. Indians of North America—Alaska.] I. Title.
E99.H2 B53 2001  971.1'004972—dc21  00-022225
Printed in Italy
6 5 4 3 2

Cover photos: Raymond Bial

The photographs in this book are used by permission and through the courtesy of: British Columbia Archives, 1, 6, 30-31, 32, 39, 40, 43, 49, 55, 58, 60, 61, 85, 94-95, 97, 107. Raymond Bial: 8-9, 13, 18, 21, 23, 24, 26-27, 52-53, 78-79, 88, 91, 99, 100, 104-105, 110-111. Museum of New Mexico: La Roche: 70327, 34; 70333, 37; Underwood & Underwood, 106392, 72. University of British Columbia: 65, 66, 69, 82, 102, 103, 117.

This book is dedicated to the Haida,
who have enriched our lives with
their striking art.

# Contents

# Author's Note

$A$T THE DAWN OF THE TWENTIETH CENTURY, NATIVE Americans were thought to be a vanishing race. However, despite four hundred years of warfare, deprivation, and disease, American Indians have not gone away. Countless thousands have lost their lives, but over the course of this century the populations of native tribes have grown tremendously. Even as American Indians struggle to adapt to modern Western life, they have also kept the flame of their traditions alive—the language, religion, stories, and the everyday ways of life. An exhilarating renaissance in Native American culture is now sweeping the nation from coast to coast.

The Lifeways books depict the social and cultural life of the major nations, from the early history of native peoples in North America to their present-day struggles for survival and dignity. Historical and contemporary photographs of traditional subjects, as well as period illustrations, are blended throughout each book so that readers may gain a sense of family life in a tipi, a hogan, or a longhouse.

No single book can comprehensively portray the intricate and varied lifeways of an entire tribe, or nation. I only hope that young people will come away with a deeper appreciation for the rich tapestry of Indian culture—both then and now—and a keen desire to learn more about these first Americans.

# 1. Origins

The Haida have long made their home on the tree-covered islands off North America's northwestern coast.

FOR NINE OR TEN THOUSAND YEARS THE HAIDA HAVE MADE THEIR HOME OFF the coast of present-day British Columbia on the Queen Charlotte Islands, known as *Haida Gwaii* (HI duh gwi), and along the southern Alaskan panhandle. The Haida, whose original name *Hidery* means "the people," have long fascinated visitors—from the explorers of the late eighteenth century to anthropologists today. Early explorers found a complex society, rich in art and ritual. The people sought a balance between themselves and the spiritual world, which was represented by nature.

One early Haida story recalls *Temlaham*, an earthly paradise where people lived peacefully in the midst of plenty. The people, however, became proud and offended the animal spirits by handling salmon bones carelessly. They were punished with a great flood. In a similar story, a one-horned mountain goat was mistreated and its spirit assumed human form to punish the people. Disguised as a dancer, the goat went to the village of the offenders. As he danced, the ground shuddered, and a huge earthquake split the earth, swallowing everyone except a man who had taken pity on the goat and nurtured him to health.

Here is a story that reaches deep into the past to the very beginnings of these coastal people.

## "The First Haida"

One day, after the Great Spirit, who was known as *Ne-kilst-lass*, had made the earth ready for people, he was walking along *Nai-con*, or Long Nose, a stretch of sandy beach. There Ne-kilst-lass came upon a cockle, or clamshell, which he impregnated with his seed. About nine months later, he passed the clamshell again and heard small peeps coming from the shell.

Ne-kilst-lass drew forth six children of whom he was the father. Each of these children was both male and female, so from three of them Ne-kilst-lass removed the female sex and from three he removed the male sex. He then had three females and three males. Ne-kilst-lass placed sea snails in the abdomens of the females. Having done so, he told the six people that if they lived together in pairs they would have many children. However, the children were hairy and naked, with such long, gangly arms and legs that they could not walk upright. Only some of the children survived, but over the generations, their descendents became strong and handsome, with little body hair.

Two of the first people were the ancestors of the Haida, and from them many generations of children came to be born. However, it was very dark where the people lived, and over time, the climate became very cold. The people began to wear clothes made from animal skins. They took shelter in the rocks, away from the bitter wind, and after a while they learned to make houses. Yet Ne-kilst-lass saw that they still needed warmth and light. He had heard that a great chief who lived on an island far out in the Pacific Ocean had all the fire in the world and kept it for himself. So Ne-kilst-lass dressed himself in a coat of glistening black feathers and became the Raven who is now known as *Choo-e-ah*.

Flying out to sea, Choo-e-ah found the island and the home of the great chief. He met and spoke at length with the chief, praising his wonderful fire. Then, suddenly, he snatched a flaming branch and flew back to the mainland coast. Here, he let sparks fall from the sky onto different kinds of wood and special stone, which thereafter held the fire within themselves. The stone, known as flint, gave back the spark when struck against another rock, just as the wood also returned the fire when two sticks were rubbed together.

When Choo-e-ah reached land part of his beak was burned away. But the Haida had learned the art of firemaking. At last, thanks to the help of the Raven, they were able to warm themselves by the light of their fires on cold winter nights.

When the Haida first arrived on the Queen Charlotte Islands the surrounding ocean was in turmoil. Raging waters and rising seas washed over their coastal homes, forcing people to move inland. Haida stories vividly recount these stormy years. Yet, in time, the waters calmed, and people settled back into villages on the beach, where they lived in comfort.

Occasionally, venturesome men set off in large cedar canoes to raid or trade with other native peoples on the west coast of what is now the province of British Columbia. They sometimes paddled the ocean-going vessels as far south as the present-day states of Washington and Oregon and often took captives in war or traded for people whom they brought home as slaves. The language of the Haida was unrelated to the languages spoken by other native groups in the region. Yet culturally the Haida had much in common with the Kwakwak'wakw (Kwakiutl) and the Bella Bella of Tsimshian, both of British Columbia, and the Tlingit, who lived nearby in Alaska.

*L*iving along the coast, the Haida relied on both the land and the sea to provide food, clothing, and shelter.

**T**his map shows the land and water along the northwestern coast of Canada where the Haida flourished for countless generations.

The open seas, the shore, and the rivers running with salmon supplied their northern home with ready food, as did the forests where the men hunted and the women gathered. From towering red cedar trees and other plant materials the Haida made canoes and stately homes, as well as tools, rope, and fibers for cloth. With the plenty around them, they had little need for agriculture.

Nor did they have to devote a great deal of time to hunting, fishing, and gathering. The Haida were liberated from the demands of day-to-day survival faced by other native people. During the long and rainy but otherwise mild winters, people had the time to refine and perfect their talent as artists. Like all the Northwest coast tribes, the Haida excelled most in the arts, especially as woodcarvers. They devoted themselves to carving and painting giant totem poles, boats, chests, and masks. They have also been noted for their large cedar-plank houses.

Haida villages typically faced the sea, with totem poles prominently representing the families who lived within each house. On the Queen Charlotte Islands they built their homes on narrow strips of land with dark cedar trees rising behind them. Some Haida came to live in present-day Alaska, having been driven away from the islands by intertribal warfare. At the time of their migration there were about eight thousand people living in five villages at the southern edge of Prince of Wales Island, which lies just north of the Queen Charlotte Islands.

For thousands of years, the Haida relied upon the land and water to provide them with food, clothing, and shelter. However, from the moment of first contact with Europeans near the end of the eighteenth century, the Haida way of life changed tragically. They began to do business with Spanish, British, and Russian traders, exchanging furs and skins for iron kettles, tools, weapons, and cloth. Many Haida adopted the whites' way of life, even as others struggled unsuccessfully to maintain their traditions. Songs, dances, and myths faded away and were forgotten. Over time, lumber mills, fisheries, and gold rushes threatened and nearly destroyed the natural environment of their homeland, along with their ancestral way of life. The Haida were also devastated by European diseases, such as the measles, for which they had no immunity. By the early 1900s the Haida faced extinction. However, over the course of the twentieth century, their population has steadily grown. In an effort to recover from the damage of the past three centuries, people have also begun to search for their cultural roots. They have begun to look hopefully into the past for a clear path to a brighter future.

## The People and the Land

Within the exceptionally rich land and sea of Haida Gwaii, a fascinating culture and sophisticated society flourished over thousands of years. For countless generations, the Haida have lived on this archipelago, about 50 miles off the coast of Canada, near its border with Alaska. Their homeland includes an isolated group of over 150 islands, both large and small, scattering over nearly four thousand square miles. The southern islands of Haida Gwaii are high and mountainous, especially Moresby Island. Most people now live on

Graham Island, the largest northern island, which is mountainous on its western side but fairly flat on the eastern shore, with craggy rocks jutting out to the sea. The Haida of Alaska, known as the Kaigani Haida, make their home north of Dixon Entrance. Their territory includes the southern half of Prince of Wales Island in Alaska.

The earliest name for the archipelago is translated as "islands coming out of concealment." Among the Haida, the preferred name is Haida Gwaii, meaning, "islands of the people." They came to be known as the Queen Charlotte Islands in 1787 when George Dixon, a British fur trader, named the islands after Queen Charlotte, the wife of the King of England, George III. Today, however, the name Queen Charlotte is beginning to be replaced by Haida Gwaii in everyday use, and the Council of the Haida Nation has recently petitioned to make the change official.

Perched on the very edge of the continental shelf in the Pacific Ocean, Haida Gwaii is washed by both icy cold northern currents full of plant and animal life and warm offshore currents originating in distant Baja, California. The blending of these waters results in a remarkable abundance—both in the sea and in the forest. Isolated from the rest of Canada, Haida Gwaii is referred to as the Canadian Galápagos because of the variety of animals and plants. On the rugged and remote islands, several unique plants, lichens, and mosses have evolved. Flowering plants, such as the alpine lily, flourish in high meadows, as do the Stellar's jay and the hairy woodpecker. Other animals, including the black bear and ermine, are rare subspecies found only on the islands.

*A*long the inlets and tree-lined coves of the Queen Charlotte Islands, the Haida built their communities.

Giant red cedars, Sitka spruce, western hemlock, and yellow cypress thrive in the cool, moist climate of the coast. Though large portions of these forests were recently threatened, in 1987 the Haida succeeded in outlawing industrial logging, and much of their land has been preserved in its natural state. Gwaii Haanas National Park Reserve and Haida Heritage Site protect the southern third of the archipelago. The towering giants in these forests are now among the last remaining old-growth trees on Earth.

The collection of islands also provides a coastal shoreline of about four thousand miles—an ideal habitat for a great variety of marine animals, including whales, porpoises, and seals. The variety of creatures in the waters along the coast is the richest in Canada, with more than three thousand species of invertebrates and four hundred kinds of fish.

Huge numbers of birds of the sea and shore live on Haida Gwaii—fully a quarter of all nesting seabirds in the Canadian Pacific—up to half a million breeding pairs each year. These include the rhinoceros auklet, Cassin's auklet, the ancient murrelet, and the tufted puffin. The islands offer nesting and feeding places for large flocks of ducks, geese, loons, and other birds. There are numerous seabird breeding colonies. Around 70,000 seabirds and waterfowl winter in the region. A quarter of Canada's rare Peale's peregrine falcon live in Gwaii Haanas. Seabirds—especially murrelets and petrels—are this falcon's favorite prey. The falcons will fly great distances, even several miles out to sea, to attack flocks of murrelets.

Large numbers of bald eagles nest in South Moresby where they can prey on a wealth of seabirds and marine animals. The trees are large enough to support their nests, which may weigh as much as 4,000 pounds. The islands are also a crucial stopover for waterfowl migrating along the Pacific flyway. Trumpeter swans and sandhill cranes are among the endangered birds that find refuge in Haida Gwaii.

The Haida understood the need for balance in nature. According to an ancient belief, "everything depends on everything else." Their survival was tightly bound to the land and the sea. From the ocean came traditional foods, including cod, halibut, and tuna. The Haida also harvested seaweeds, fished for herring, and caught salmon at river mouths. The Nass and Skeena rivers on the mainland are home to all five species of Pacific salmon, as well as to steelhead trout, and today support large commercial salmon fisheries. Along the archipelago's east coast, sheltered from the open ocean, is a rich intertidal zone. Over two hundred different kinds of animals have been found here.

The abundance of food attracts many kinds of whales, both toothed and baleen, and harbor porpoises, Dall's porpoises, and Pacific white-sided dolphins. Toothed whales prey on fish, squid, and sea mammals; baleen whales scoop up enormous mouthfuls of plankton. In Gwaii Haanas are found many species of toothed whales—killer whales, sperm whales, Curvier's beaked whales, short-finned pilot whales, and Baird's beaked whales—along with a great variety of baleens—humpbacks, gray whales, mink whales, fin whales, blue whales, sei whales, and right whales.

*Conifers grow on Haida Gwaii, thriving in the warm, moist climate of the Pacific Northwest.*

The Haida feasted on whales stranded on the beach, and hunted seals, sea otters, and sea lions for meat, hides, and sinew. Harbor seals and Steller sea lions lounged on the rocky shores. Over half of British Columbia's sea lion population thrives in the plankton-rich waters of Haida Gwaii. A large sea lion rookery is situated on Cape St. James at the southern tip of Gwaii Haanas. There are also several "haul-outs" in the area. Sea lions are especially vulnerable from late May to mid-July when cows, or mothers, are giving birth. They pick birthing places high on the rocks of Haida Gwaii to protect the young from being swept away in the crashing waves. Their pups are utterly helpless for the first two weeks after birth. If the mother is frightened, she will try to move the pup and so run the risk of its falling into cracks in the rocks or drowning in the ocean. Boats must stay away from the rookery during this time.

Much of the life of Gwaii Haanas is found in underwater forests of giant and bull kelp. Anchored to the ocean floor with a holdfast, the kelp's pliable stalks reach toward the sunlight at the surface, draping a sheltering roof over sea creatures below. Hundreds of species of fish and invertebrates live among the kelp's leaves. Some predators hide in the fronds to surprise unwary prey. Marine mammals, notably sea lions and harbor seals, relax and sometimes hunt in the kelp forest. Bat stars, snails, and anemones feed on drift-fronds that have broken off from the main plant.

Parks Canada and the Department of Fisheries and Oceans are working with the Council of Haida Nations to establish the Gwaii Haanas Marine Conservation Area, which will protect the sur-

Many different species are found in the coastal waters, including this starfish in a tide pool among the rocks.

*The Haida were highly skilled seafarers. Trading with mainland groups meant braving the unpredictable ocean.*

rounding waters as well as the land of Haida Gwaii. Recently, four oil companies gave up their right to drill within the proposed boundaries of the conservation area.

The Haida relationship with the ocean reaches far back in time. Until the turn of the nineteenth century, the Haida plied the ocean in impressive canoes. Carved from giant red cedars, with planks steamed into graceful shapes, these canoes extended the Haida economy and culture by allowing offshore fishing, sea mammal hunting, and long distance travel. The sixty-foot-long canoes were the most prized ocean craft of the north Pacific coast and the major item traded by the Haida with their native neighbors on the mainland.

The culture was preserved not only in song and dance, carved images, language and stories but through the experience of waking, living, and sleeping again on the islands. To live on Haida Gwaii meant following the seasons—of herring spawns and salmon runs. People felt the air, misty and moist, as they prepared fish for the smokehouse or strolled over green moss in the forest. Feelings for the land and sea deepened when people faced winter storms and took joy in the occasional sunlight. In a single moment while carving a totem or digging for clams, they experienced their heritage and gave thanks for their well-being.

# 2. At Home on the Sea

This totem pole on the front of a Haida house was carved by the artists Bill Reid and Doug Cranmer.

TRACES OF HAIDA ANCESTORS HAVE BEEN FOUND AT OVER EIGHT HUNDRED sites on Haida Gwaii. The oldest of these places reveals that people have lived on the islands for at least nine thousand years. At that time, a grassy plain covered much of the Hecate Straits, which now separate the islands from the Canadian mainland. People and animals moved freely back and forth. There were lakes and small rivers flowing north and south to the Pacific Ocean, and many areas were inhabited. Among the first traces of the Haida are roughly flaked stone tools found in intertidal waters that were once dry land. These tools were made of obsidian, a volcanic glass found on the mainland. Their presence on Haida Gwaii is evidence of the maritime skills of these ancient people, who were able to paddle their ocean-going canoes long distances to visit neighbors.

Melting glaciers caused the ocean to rise gradually and flood many of the coastal lands—well above the high tide marks of today. The dramatic rise in sea levels has been remembered over the generations in many flood stories of native people along the Northwest coast, including the Haida. These stories point to their having inhabited the islands since the end of the last ice age, making them one of the oldest populations in North America. In 1892, James Deans, a Hudson's Bay Company trader, was told this story about glacial shifts at the Hunnah River on Haida Gwaii:

At Quilh-ca, about three miles west from the village of Illth-cah-geetla, or Skidegate's town, lived a boy whose name was Scannah-gan-nuncus. One day, making a venture further than usual, he sailed up the Honna, a mountain stream emptying its waters into Skidegate channel, four or five miles west from the place where he lived. Tradition says that this river in those days was three times larger than it is nowadays. At present there is seldom water enough to float a canoe, unless at high water. It is also related that the waters of the sea stood higher on the land than is now the case. Of the rise of the land, evidence is everywhere to be seen; old landmarks show thirty feet.

After pulling up stream, he became tired; so, in order to rest, he pulled ashore and lay down. In those days at the place where he went ashore were large boulders in the bed of the stream, while on both sides of the river were many trees.

While resting by the river, he heard a dreadful noise up stream, coming toward him. Looking to see what it was, he was surprised to behold all the stones in the river coming toward him. The movement of the stones frightened him so much that he jumped to his feet and ran into the timber. Here he found he had made a mistake, because all the trees were cracking and groaning; all seemed to say to him, "Go back, go back at once to the river, and run as fast as you can." This he lost no time doing.

When again at the river, led by his curiosity, he went to see what was crushing the stones and breaking the trees. On reaching them, he found that a large body of ice was coming

down, pushing everything before it. Seeing this, he got into
his canoe and fled toward home.

AS EARLY AS FIVE THOUSAND YEARS AGO, THERE WAS A SUBSTANTIAL POPU-
lation on Haida Gwaii, where the Haida of Canada continue to live
today. But in ancient times people were more widely scattered
throughout the archipelago. According to early fur traders, many

**A**s shown in this diorama of a busy coastal village, the Haida prospered on
their collection of islands.

people lived in the south at Skungwai, or Ninstints, and in the north at Cloak Bay, where several villages were clustered. These included Kiusta, Dadens, and Yaku. On Masset Inlet were the major villages of Masset, Yan, and Kayung. On Skidegate Inlet lay the village of Skidegate. The Haida chose sites that sheltered them from the winter storms that hammered the Pacific coast and Hecate Strait.

Although people lived most of the year in these villages, they left for streams or rivers whenever there was a fish run. They relied

*T*he Haida devoted considerable time to creating works of art, including elaborately carved totem poles, which towered over their villages.

heavily on salmon for food, but the fish ran only every other year. So the Haida established rights to the rich halibut runs and on the west coast they caught black cod. People also gathered clams and other shellfish. A kind of oil-rich herring, known as eulachon, was not found on Haida Gwaii, so the Haida journeyed to the enormous runs on the Nass River on the mainland. While there, they also traded for other foods and art materials not found in their archipelago.

Newton H. Chittenden, a surveyor for the British Columbia provincial government, visited several Haida villages and reported:

> All the villages named are beautifully situated, facing the south from cozy sheltered nooks, with splendid beaches, and abundant supplies of food conveniently near. Besides the halibut bank marked on the chart, there is one near all of the villages mentioned, and inexhaustible quantities of clams and mussels along the neighboring shores. This is certainly one of the most favored regions in the world for the abode of the Indian.

In the 1700s, some families began to move from overpopulated villages around North Island to what is today known as the Prince of Wales archipelago in southeast Alaska. They wished to be nearer the Russian trading posts at Wrangell and Sitka, which offered new objects of wealth, and to live in a less crowded area. According to traders' accounts of the late eighteenth century, so many families moved from Dadens village on Haida Gwaii that the community was

*B*uilt of sturdy beams and planks, cedar houses shared the rocky beach with painted totem poles.

virtually abandoned by the early nineteenth century. Gradually, the Kaigani Haida, as they came to be known, displaced the Tlingit-speaking people who had lived in the Prince of Wales archipelago for thousands of years. Yet some of the ancestral Tlingit place names survived in many Kaigani Haida villages.

## Villages

Haida villages consisted of one or two rows of houses strung along the beach. Double-row villages were common, and there may have been villages with up to five rows of houses in ancient times. Generally, the chief owned the largest house, which stood in the middle of the village.

Their complex society was hierarchical, with classes of commoners and nobles, slaves and *skaggy*, or medicine men. Upper classes, or nobles, owned hunting and gathering rights near Haida villages. Commoners had to pay to hunt, fish, or gather in these places. Some commoners enjoyed prestige as artists, mask and canoe makers, shamans, and as relatives of the chief. Other commoners were simply considered lower-class citizens, while slaves, with no rights, were scarcely considered part of Haida society. Captured in raids and warfare with other tribes, slaves were always men or boys. They were forced to do the most menial chores around the village. Yet if they proved themselves skilled as craftsmen, hunters, and fishermen they might someday be freed and honored for their ability. Eventually, the Canadian government outlawed slavery among the Haida and other coastal peoples.

## Cedar-Plank Houses

Haida longhouses ranged in size from twenty to thirty feet to large houses up to fifty by sixty feet. Fifteen to twenty family members might live in a cedar-plank house, while a large dwelling provided shelter for twice as many occupants, including the families and their slaves. The chief and his immediate family slept in the back of the house. Here, there might also be a separate room with an oval entrance. Other family groups living in the house made partitions for their quarters, sometimes with carved and painted boxes that held their belongings

Made of wood, these houses were much more complicated than those of most other Native American groups. Traditionally, the house was considered one of the principal gifts of the Raven to the Haida people—after he stole the knowledge of home building from the Beaver. Families shared the fireplace where meals were prepared and then retired to their own sleeping areas. The center of social, political, and economic life, the highly decorated house was where the Haida created and used their art.

Built of western red cedar, the frame consisted of sturdy corner posts that supported the massive roof beams. To make the frame, men laid cedar logs notched and fitted together so skillfully that pegs were not needed. They sheathed the frame with broad split-cedar planks and covered the roof with slabs of cedar bark. Men used adzes, mauls, and wedges for splitting the wood. A tool might be art-fully decorated, such as an elaborately carved basalt maul for driving wood wedges into red cedar logs to split off planks. The roofs of high-ranking people were shingled with overlapping planks held down with heavy rocks. The houses of poor people and canoe sheds had cedar-bark roofs that had to be replaced often.

Men used opulently carved and painted wood pillars to help support the roof beams, which made the oval entrances more

**O**ver time, the Haida established settlements in Alaska. These mortuary columns, shown in a photograph taken around 1900, are on the west side of the village of Kasaan.

impressive. Over time, the beams evolved into a variety of totem poles, some of which were fifty feet tall. The clan symbol, either the raven or the eagle, was featured on a pole, along with family crests—animals, birds, sea creatures, and mythic beings. The meaning of these crests lay in stories of the Haida's origin. The crest might refer to daily chores, family customs, or beliefs as well. Totem poles also depicted major events in the lives of the family heads. Some totem poles even held the remains of the deceased members of the household. Only the nobles could have totem poles; commoners were only allowed to paint images on their houses.

House styles varied by region. In the villages of the Prince of Wales archipelago, houses resembled the large gable-roofed plank structures often found along the north coast. The frame consisted of four or more heavy vertical posts spanned by massive round beams up to fifty feet long, which were clad with wide planks. In the south, notably in the village of Ninstints at the southern tip of Haida Gwaii, the plank cladding fit precisely between parallel timbers of the frame. This refined style of house, with nearly perfect carpentry, likely did not develop until steel tools became available in the late 1700s. A third kind of house often found among the Kaigani Haida had both an interior frame of four massive posts and walls and gables supported by four smaller exterior corner posts. Large houses, like that of Chief Skowl at Kasaan village, relied on a massive horizontal timber between the front corner posts.

The house was warmed by a central hearth—a large fire pit often framed with massive vertical planks. Directly above was a smokehole, which had a plank flap. This flap could be moved with ropes to control the draft for the fire.

Decorated wood partitions created sleeping compartments and offered a little privacy. During ceremonies, additional canvas screens painted with crest designs were placed to the back of the house to form a drop behind which dancers could put on their costumes. Storage boxes were stacked around the walls of the house, with formal seats reserved for the chief and his wives.

*These cedar houses, built in a row on Maude Island, each feature a tall frontal totem pole.*

**H**eavy carved timbers provided a strong framework for the roof and walls of a cedar house.

The chief's seat of honor was placed on a platform in the center of the house facing the door. This seat—a box decorated with the crest of the chief—was thought to protect the spirit of the chief. The decoration was on the inside so that the public viewed the chief surrounded by his crests.

The Haida erected their longhouses on sites that offered protection from the weather and enemy attack. During the salmon run in the spring they moved to camps along the rivers. Occasionally, they removed cedar planks from the walls to make shelters, then brought the planks back in the fall. They might lash the planks across two canoes to make a platform for carrying their belongings. Separate quarters were built for girls who were coming of age and for women about to give birth. Other buildings housed the remains of the dead, and large community buildings were put up for celebrations, such as spirit dances.

Ensign Albert Niblack first visited Haida villages during his tours of duty with the U.S. Navy. Later, in the 1880s, he returned for a number of years to photograph Haida dwellings and gather information about them for the Smithsonian Institution. He said, "Their houses are exceptionally well constructed, and the custom of erecting the carved column in contact with the front of the house and cutting a circular doorway through both, seems to be nowhere so universally practiced."

## Families and Clans

Haida society was matrilineal, which means children traced their descent through the mother's side of the family. A man inherited wealth through his mother's side and his social rank through his mother's brother, who served as family head. A chief, for example, usually inherited his title from his mother's brother—his maternal uncle. Property, titles, names, crests, masks, performances, and even songs were among the hereditary privileges. A group of related families descending from a common ancestor formed a lineage, or family line. The Haida did not wage war with villages of the same lineage and were hospitable to members in the extended family, whether they were acquainted or not. During the warm months, men worked to amass more wealth, which enhanced their status. They displayed their wealth in feasts known as potlatches. The term potlatch comes from the Nootka word *patshatl*, meaning "to give away."

Made up of about ten closely related nuclear families of the same lineage, each household generally included between thirty and forty people. The house was headed by a chief. However, the houses of powerful chiefs were often larger, with up to a hundred individuals. Each lineage also recognized the authority of another chief who would lead them in times of war. Inherited positions determined the order in which chiefs or other people of high rank were seated at potlatches and other feasts.

The most important of the Haida's ceremonies was the potlatch. The building of a house and the raising of its frontal pole might become a major occasion for hosting a potlatch. A high-ranking man might devote years to gathering great wealth so that he could lavish gifts and enormous amounts of food upon his guests. Those who had never given a potlatch or who did not own a house or major property were considered commoners. Many Haida owned slaves, who were captives from war or the children of captives taken from neighboring tribes on Vancouver Island or the mainland.

All families belonged to either of two large social groups, or moieties, known as Raven and Eagle. Within each moiety, members of a particular lineage lived at opposite ends of the village and chose mar-

Members of the Eagle moiety, or group, often depicted this revered bird in their works of art.

riage partners from the other group. One could not marry a member of one's social group; an Eagle had to marry a Raven, and vice versa.

Families controlled many resources, such as locations for fishing, hunting, and collecting sea creatures, as well as sites for building homes. People also owned an abundance of myths and legends, dances, songs, and musical compositions. Even names were highly desired as property and were bestowed to acknowledge different stages of a person's life. People gave names to cherished belongings, such as fish traps, houses, canoes, feast dishes, and spoons. Designs used for face painting and tattoos were also considered property of the family, as were the seventy crests of the Haida.

Clans were made up of a number of houses belonging to either the Eagle or the Raven group. Each clan was represented by both its own crest and that of the Eagle or the Raven. These crests were thought to have been obtained by the ancestors of the clan through an encounter with an animal spirit. Rights to a crest could also be acquired through marriage, as a gift, in war, or by the extinction of the clan. Clans frequently displayed their crests. The most prestigious house was that of the clan chief. All of the clan chiefs in a village formed a council, and the head chief among them served as leader of the village.

The Raven was made up of twenty-two families and the Eagle of twenty-three. Members of the two groups often helped each other. For example, if an Eagle chief died, the Ravens arranged the funeral, after which the Eagles would reward them with a potlatch. When a child was born, the other social group crafted a cradle, and if a Raven needed a new house, the Eagles arranged to build it. In return, they received presents from the Ravens when the house was dedicated.

The head of the most wealthy or populous lineage in the community became the town chief. He remained in charge only so long as he won respect and his lineage kept its wealth. The competition for this position could become fierce. Over the last century, for example, there was intense rivalry between two leaders—Chief Ninsingwas and Chief Skidegate. According to Newton H. Chittenden, the nineteenth century surveyor, "They quarreled bitterly over their rank for a long time, Ning-Ging-Wash (Ninsingwas), by means of his more liberal potlatches finally prevailing, but not until two of their adherents had been killed."

To this day, Haida society depends upon leadership by a chief and the division into clans. Relationships shift between conflict and resolution. All Haida are either Raven or Eagle and trace their descent through their mother.

## Mythology and Crests

Most Haida objects are decorated with crests of the Raven or the Eagle along with the symbol of the owner's lineage. The smaller figures attached to the crest by the ears, chest, or mouth often refer to a specific myth involving that crest. For example, on the chest of the Raven the prominent Edenshaw family depicts the Butterfly, Raven's traveling companion throughout a series of stories as told by the Masset. In the Skidegate stories, however, it is the Eagle who accompanies the Raven on his journeys. Since the Haida have thou-

Crests were skillfully carved on totem poles. These figures related the history of the family lineage.

sands of myths from which to choose, it is nearly impossible to understand the full meaning of the symbols on a totem pole. Moreover, there is no longer anyone alive who is familiar with the range and breadth of these stories, whether depicted on tattoos or totem poles.

Although the Haida have almost seventy crest figures, fewer than twenty are now used. Some belonged to many lineages, while a large number were the exclusive property of a few families. The Killer Whale, for example, is an especially strong and popular feature of Haida art and mythology. All Raven lineages have forms of the Killer Whale as a crest. One of these, the Raven-Finned Killer Whale, symbolizes the story in which the Raven pecked himself out of the body of the Killer Whale through the end of its dorsal fin. Eagle lineages of Ninstints used only the Five-Finned Killer Whale, which connected them to Killer Whale chiefs whose undersea village was located nearby and with whom their ancestors enjoyed a profitable relationship. The tall dorsal fin of Killer Whale crests that belong to Ravens are always black, while those of Eagles include a diagonal white stripe.

All the land mammals in crests, except the Beaver, belong to the Ravens. Some of these, such as the Mountain Goat, the Wolf, and the Grizzly, are not found on Haida Gwaii. These crests came from Tsimshian chiefs on the mainland. Most crests of water creatures, including the Beaver and the Frog, are the exclusive property of the Eagles. They also originated with the Tsimshian. Sea animals primarily belong to the Ravens, although many Eagles have the

Blackfish as a crest. Most fish crests, including the Sculpin, Skate, Dogfish, Starfish, and Halibut belong to the Eagles.

Curiously, the Ravens do not make use of the Raven as a crest, but the Eagles do have this trickster, along with many other bird crests including the Cormorant, Heron, Hawk, and Hummingbird. The only bird crests of the Ravens are the Flicker, Hawk, and Horned Owl.

## Potlatches

A chief usually held a potlatch to celebrate a major event—the death of his predecessor, the naming of a child, a child's coming of age, a marriage, or the unveiling of a new totem pole. Lower-ranking nobles also hosted potlatches to acknowledge major events in their lives. A big potlatch might be planned for several years. The most extravagant potlatches, including secret society initiations, were held during the winter when the Haida had more leisure time. Sometimes referred to as "fighting with property," potlatches drew guests from a wide area.

Arriving in their finest canoes, the guests might include people of the host's own clan and people from neighboring villages. Guests came singing with their clan crest displayed in the bow of the canoe. They continued to sing and dance as they made their way to the feast house. Guests were seated around the hearth where the gifts were displayed. Seating was arranged by rank, which could be challenged if a guest thought his place did not reflect his social position.

Haida chiefs improved their social position by hosting potlatches during which they displayed—and gave away—much of their wealth.

During the feast, which went on for several days, the host gave away or destroyed possessions to impress others. The more the host was able to give away, the higher his status rose, because he could afford to lose so much wealth. He presented his guests with gifts in accordance with their social standing. Accepting a gift indicated approval of the host's high position. Canoes, baskets, cloaks woven from bark fibers and mountain goat wool, blankets, and ornaments were given away. Among the most precious gifts was oolichan oil; chiefs even traded their canoes to obtain this oil for a potlatch. Hosts also lavished piles of Chilkat blankets made from goat's wool on their guests, which could only be had at a high price on the mainland.

The more generous the host the higher his esteem, and the guests were expected to consume as much food as possible. Guests were presented with huge bowls of seal or bear meat and berries preserved in fish oil. If the visitors could not eat all the food, they were embarrassed and might be ridiculed by the host. At the conclusion of the potlatch, the host was left impoverished. Yet it was expected that his generosity would be repaid in double, so he might eventually receive two gifts for every one he had bestowed on others. Amid the feasting and presenting of gifts, speakers praised the host and mocked the guests, especially if they couldn't eat enough or didn't show enough appreciation for their gifts. During potlatches, people recalled their family history, telling about the acquisition of hereditary privileges, names, and crests.

Potlatches also gave the host an opportunity to show off his abundance of useful and artfully crafted possessions, including feast bowls and utensils adorned with crests and carvings. In turn, guests impressed others by eating as much as possible. Serving dishes, bowls, bentwood, trays, ladles, and spoons in many shapes and sizes were set out at a feast. Well-crafted pieces drew high praise from the guests.

Artists carved dishes and bowls from solid blocks of wood. They also shaped these objects from horn, softened by steam, or bent wooden boards into box shapes, then pegged or sewed the joints. Vessels made along the northern coast were particularly distinctive—both useful and as lovely as the finest sculpture.

# 3. Lifeways

With a wealth of trees in the surrounding forest, Haida artists turned blocks of wood into elaborate works of art.

IN THEIR HOMES ALONG THE SEASHORE, THE HAIDA LIVED IN HARMONY WITH the cycle of the seasons and the generations, and children were especially valued. According to a popular Haida saying, "We do not inherit the earth from our ancestors, we borrow it from our children." Almost every child was believed to be the reincarnation of a dead ancestor. The family knew the ancestor by birth marks, physical features, personality traits, or comments by the child about past memories. Although born in a certain class, any boy or girl who saved and worked hard might rise to the highest rank among the Haida. If given an ugly name at birth that shamed them, they strived to earn a better name. If they acquired wealth and held a potlatch, the chief would reward them with a good and honorable name.

## Cycle of Life

**Birth.** Pregnant women observed a number of taboos and underwent a variety of rituals to ensure a healthy baby and easy delivery. A woman related to the family of the father assisted the mother in childbirth and welcomed the newborn baby into the world. The Haida delighted in the birth of a child, whether a boy or a girl, although they favored girls, who would carry on the family lineage.

The parents named their newborns after a person in the paternal grandfather's family, usually at a small feast. When babies were very young, perhaps four days old, they had their ears pierced. Over the years, they pierced their ears more times and had their bodies tattooed—the arms, legs, chest, and back of men and the arms and legs of women.

**Childhood.** Fathers instructed their sons, but at an early age the boys went to live with their mother's brothers, who also helped with their training. Boys learned their family heritage as well as proper conduct in Haida society. The uncles toughened up the boys by making them swim in the cold ocean during the winter. Although they had no puberty rituals, boys were required to eat dragonfly wings to become fast swimmers and to suck on the beaks of diving ducks to have strong lungs underwater.

*Though these young women wear modern dress and live in a Western-style village, they have been raised to honor their role within Haida society—and pass on its traditions to their children.*

Mothers took responsibility for their daughters, instructing them to fill their roles in the Haida community. They taught the girls the many tasks of managing a household, including cooking meals, making clothing, and taking care of children. Mothers also showed their daughters how to gather spruce root, cedar bark, and berries in the forest and how to harvest seaweed from the ocean.

**Coming-of-Age.** A girl of a high-ranking family had her lower lip pierced so she could wear a labret, or lip ornament, made from wood, bone, or walrus ivory. Each year she received a larger labret, whose size reflected her social position.

When a girl had her first menstrual cycle, she was secluded behind a screen in the back corner of her parents' house. The higher her rank the longer she was isolated. To strengthen herself, she lay her head on a stone pillow, ate very little food, and drank no water. She could not approach the central fire because it was believed that her face would turn permanently red.

The girl was not allowed to talk or laugh during this time. When she left the house, she could not use the main door. Hunting and fishing gear, as well as objects for gambling, were kept away from her to avoid contamination. During this time, her aunts (the sisters of her father) looked after her. At the end of her period, they ritually cleansed the girl. The family then held a feast to honor her entry into womanhood, and the mother gave property to the father's sisters. For the next two to five years, taboos were observed at each period, and the young woman continued to go into brief seclusion.

**Marriage.** Marriages were arranged among the Haida, often during the couple's childhood—and during infancy in Skidegate. Parents made the arrangements if the betrothed were very young. If the couple were older, members of the man's family met with the girl's parents and often her maternal uncle. For both men and women, someone of the father's family was favored as a mate. At the wedding, the parents of the couple exchanged gifts. The groom offered property to the bride's maternal uncles, and in turn, the woman's uncles and father gave property to the husband. Although everyone feasted at the marriage, this exchange of gifts was not considered a potlatch.

**Death.** Of all rituals, death ceremonies were the most elaborate. And the higher the rank of the deceased the greater their complexity. The women of the deceased father's family cleansed and dressed the body, then painted the face. Amidst a display of personal property, the body lay in state for several days at the rear of the cedar house. Family and friends filed past the body to pay their respects and sing crying songs.

Men of the father's family built a coffin. The body was placed inside and carried from the house. The body was placed in a family grave house that kept out the damp and rain. The body was usually moved later to lie beneath a newly carved mortuary column. Sometimes a memorial pole was put up, and the body remained in the grave house. A man's mortuary potlatch was then held by the heir of the deceased, while a woman's was given by her husband.

*T*his photograph depicts the impressive tomb at Yan in the Queen Charlotte Islands, where the remains of a chief are buried.

Commoners were not usually placed in grave houses with those of high rank, and carved poles were not erected in their honor. At death, slaves were cast into the sea.

When a man died, his younger brothers and nephews took his property. Often the house was literally cleaned out, leaving the widow with only her cooking utensils and personal property. The property of a deceased woman went to her daughters. To mourn a death, the spouse fasted for several days, and relatives and friends cut their hair and blackened their faces with pitch.

Often, as death approached, individuals expressed a reincarnation promise, sometimes naming the parent to whom they would be reborn. At death, it was believed that the deceased was carried by canoe to the Land of Souls.

## Hunting, Fishing, and Gathering

From one season to another, the ancestors of the Haida went to sea to fish and wandered the land to hunt and gather wild plants. During the warm summer months, they paddled by canoe to rivers—crystal clear and cold—to catch sockeye salmon. Their gear included nets, as well as hooks and lines and underwater traps called weirs. So many salmon ran the rivers in the spring that the Haida could also catch them by hand. Families still journey to the Yakoun River and Copper Bay to fish for sockeye. Dried, frozen, canned, or smoked, the summer harvest is eaten throughout the year. Preserved seafood is often served at the many winter feasts. A family who gives away these traditional foods is still considered rich and generous.

For thousands of years, the Haida also caught fish such as cod and herring in the Pacific. They caught halibut and sturgeon so large they had to be clubbed before they could be dragged into their canoes. Although they hunted seals, sea lions, and otters, they did not pursue whales, only feasting upon those that washed ashore. They loved shellfish and harvested oysters and mussels.

**H**aida children grew up by the ocean and learned how to fish the coastal waters.

*In the traditional way of drying fish, fillets are hung from the rafters, as in this building in the community of Old Masset.*

In the forest, they brought down deer, caribou, land otters, and black bear. They raided bird nests for eggs and gathered fruits, nuts, and berries, according to the season.

The Haida knew that their environment had to be respected if they were to have bountiful harvests year after year. They always gave thanks for the foods provided to them. In recent years when logging and mining damaged the water, soil, and trees of Haida Gwaii, the Haida have fought to recover and preserve the delicate balance of nature for future generations.

## Food Preparation

To this day, the Haida relish the traditional seafood of their home-land. During the spring and summer, people in coastal communities come together to busily prepare salmon, halibut, and seaweeds harvested from the Pacific Ocean. Returning to the rivers and oceans strengthens a sense of community and spiritual renewal. Food has always been at the center of Haida social life. When families come together to harvest food, everyone is happy. Ernie Collison remembers the old people as "always laughing and teasing each other and having a lot of fun. Part of the enjoyment came from the food we gathered from the waters and the land." Herring roe, or eggs, served on kelp, is a favorite among the Haida. Known as *k'aaw*, this dish is a delicacy sought around the world.

Haida women prepare another delicious food in their kitchens—razor clams. At the start of clam-digging season, everyone in the village of Old Massett heads to Tow Hill, often for the whole day. Families frequently picnic together as they dig clams. One woman recalled, "When I was a child, my uncle used to pay me five dollars for a day's work of stomping in the sand to summon the clams, and picking up the clams that he dug. When we got home, I learned how to clean clams by watching my *naanii* (grandmother), mom and aunts."

## Art

The Haida fashioned for themselves a rich world of costumes and adornments and everyday objects. However, the Haida did not create "art for art's sake." In fact, there is no word for "art" in the Haida lan-

# Salmon Patties

1 16 oz can pink salmon, bones and skin removed (reserve liquid)

2 beaten eggs

$\frac{1}{2}$ cup chopped onion

2 tablespoons butter

$\frac{2}{3}$ cup fine dry bread crumbs

1 teaspoon dried dillweed

$\frac{1}{2}$ teaspoon dried mustard

2 tablespoons cooking oil


Drain salmon, reserving the liquid. Discard bones and skin; flake meat.

Sauté onion in butter until tender. Remove from heat.

Add salmon liquid, $\frac{1}{3}$ cup of the bread crumbs, eggs, dillweed, mustard, and salmon.

Mix well and shape into four patties, then coat with remaining crumbs.

Heat oil in a skillet and cook patties over medium heat about three minutes on each side, or until nicely browned.

guage. Their art reflected their spiritual beliefs. Every work of art expressed the social status and rights bestowed on their ancestors by supernatural beings or taught to them in mythic encounters with the animals, birds, fish, or other beings. The images of these creatures were embodied in the crests handed down through generations.

Demanding the highest standards of craftsmanship and continually seeking to refine their work, they lived in the midst of their art. Their art was sustained by the natural resources of Haida Gwaii: cedar to carve totem poles, canoes, and masks; cedar bark and spruce roots to fashion hats; and shells to decorate button blankets and masks.

About two thousand years ago these inhabitants of an isolated archipelago began to trade their work, especially their remarkable canoes, with their coastal neighbors. They also gave carved and painted chests and other furnishings to Northwest peoples in exchange for mineral pigments, special stones, and metals. They turned these raw materials into objects and traded them back to tribes on Vancouver Island and the mainland. These finely crafted objects included copper shields, horn bowls, ladles, spoons, and perhaps goat's wool blankets. The Haida were skilled in fashioning and engraving copper shields, which they traded to the Tsimshian, Tlingit, Kwakiutl, and other peoples. In the late eighteenth century, they also began to make and trade silver and copper jewelry.

For the Haida, art was created not only to satisfy the artist, but to impress others—and every surface was either painted or carved with designs. Totem poles, house posts, grave markers and mortuary

*T*his wooden bear sculpture by Bill Reid displays the fine craftsmanship for which the Haida have long been known.

poles, painted houses, interior screens, enormous feast dishes, and canoes all reflected ancestry, status, and wealth. Small objects such as ceremonial costumes, headdresses, helmets, speaker staffs, rattles, serving implements, eating utensils, boxes, and containers were also forms of creative expression.

Ranging in size from tiny insects to whales, many animal symbols are used in Haida art, notably the raven, eagle, bear, and wolf. The raven and eagle were—and still are—the most prominent animals in

**W**ood-carvers produced impressive masks, such as this piece decorated in the Haida style.

Haida mythology. Masks, especially transformation masks, were a key part of many ceremonies. The Haida believed that a spirit would inhabit any mask on which it was depicted. The actions of the person wearing the mask were then guided by the spirit. Shamans, or medicine men, relied on many art objects for their rituals, including small charms of walrus ivory, bone, and animal teeth. Other ceremonial art included rattles, noisemakers, drums, puppets, and dolls.

When European traders first arrived on the islands they admired the Haida's watertight boxes decorated with symbols of ancestry and wealth and the intricate miniatures carved from a soft black stone known as argillite. The Haida began to create souvenirs for the newcomers. Among the most popular were small carvings made from argillite, items of ivory and silver, and a variety of baskets. Thousands of these objects, collected before the trade in sea otter pelts ended in the 1830s, found their way to New England and the British isles, as well as museum collections.

## Clothing and Jewelry

For many generations, the Haida have been weavers skilled at making ceremonial garments out of dog fur, mountain goat wool, and bark thread. They fashioned masks representing the eagle, salmon, and other animals, and headdresses fringed with ermine and adorned with sea lion whiskers and carvings. They also made blankets decorated with pearl buttons, which they draped over their shoulders at dances.

People tattooed themselves. Traditionally, the tattoos displayed rank through the crests of their family's clan. Young men were tattooed on their chests while women sported tattoos on their arms and legs and wore lip ornaments. Skin piercing was also common.

Over time, trade among the Haida, Tsimshian, and Tlingit led to their sharing a variety of objects and materials that symbolized wealth and prestige. These included highly decorated chests, boxes, and bowls for display at potlatches. Chiefs of all the coastal tribes owned a variety of regalia, fine articles of clothing such as headdresses decorated with ermine skins, which provided a common means of exchange among nations with different languages and belief systems. The full set of regalia included a Chilkat blanket, leggings, an apron, a frontlet, and a pair of Raven rattles (or a drum). A chief was also likely to own a shield-shaped plate of native copper that was displayed at feasts and could be exchanged. After a chief's death, his copper belongings were often attached to his memorial pole.

The Haida adopted most of these symbols of rank, especially articles of clothing, from the Tsimshian and Nisga'a. They also made their own or acquired them through trade with mainland tribes. The Haida made their own frontlets, which were bands or ornaments worn on their foreheads, and Raven rattles; they also sometimes traded for them with tribes on the mainland. People of other classes, such as shaman or members of secret societies, also had their own special regalia.

Haida chiefs were lavishly adorned. They favored fur-trimmed, bark-fiber robes, and tall hats. During the damp winters, they

$\mathbf{M}$ade by the noted artist Charles Edenshaw, this silver bracelet reflects the Haidas' appreciation for finely crafted jewelry.

donned animal skins and cedar-bark rain capes. The men often went naked indoors or during warm weather, but it was thought to be shameful for them to be seen nude by slaves. The men frequently went barefoot year round because the damp ground quickly soaked through leather moccasins.

Women usually wore short aprons and kilts or toga-like garments during the winter. The upper classes preferred fur or cedar-fiber robes worn over the shoulder, which freed one arm. The Haida also valued ceremonial Chilkat blankets, which they wore like capes. Dyed yellow, dark brown, or greenish-blue, the blankets required the wool of three mountain goats twisted by hand, spun with cedar bark, and then woven in intricate designs of birds and animals. After European contact, button blankets or beaded blankets made of wool or flannel replaced the Chilkat blankets. These blankets were often blue, with the crest animal appliquéd and outlined with mother-of-pearl buttons on the surface. Dancing capes and tunics were made of animal hide with crest designs painted on the surface. These were often fringed with hooves, which made a delicate clinking sound as the wearer moved.

Another distinctive feature of Haida regalia was ceremonial dancing headdresses worn to welcome guests at potlatches and other events. These masklike headdresses showed rank, heredity, and supernatural powers, or illustrated a belief. Headdresses also displayed a clan crest. Some headdresses served as war helmets as well. Hats not only offered protection against the rain, but indicated status, with rings for each potlatch given.

## Canoes and Trade

The canoe was essential to the Haida way of life. The jagged coastline of their island home and the bounty of the sea required water travel, frequently over rough waters. The gigantic red cedar trees harvested from deep within the temperate rain forest had the perfect grain for seaworthy vessels. Over many generations, men became unsurpassed designers and builders of canoes.

Greatly prized by chiefs of other nations along the coast, the canoes had graceful lines that not only were pleasing to the eye but allowed them to move swiftly. Throughout the autumn canoemakers worked on their new craft within reach of the best red cedars. After a snowfall, they slid the roughed-out canoes from the woods to a nearby beach and then towed the craft back to their villages. Here, they finished their work over the rest of the winter. Canoes varied in size. Some were seventy-five feet long and able to carry forty people and two tons of goods. In the spring, men took flotillas, or groups, of new canoes from Skidegate Inlet, Masset, and Rose Spit on the north coast over the stormy waters to the mainland. If their craft could cross the treacherous Hecate Strait, they knew the canoes could withstand just about any weather along the coast. They traded the canoes to coastal tribes, notably the Tsimshian, Bella Bella, and Tlingit, who had gathered to fish during the spring. The Haida accepted old canoes in trade, which they paddled back to their homes.

Men also loaded fleets of new canoes with dried halibut and strips of cedar bark and set out across the dangerous straits to trade for oolichan oil, as well as hides, meat, horns of mountain goat and

*T*he Haida continued to make large, graceful canoes well into the twentieth century, as seen in this photograph of Kasaan, Alaska.

sheep, and other goods not available on the islands. They traded for candlefish, too. These fish were so oily they could be fitted with a wick and burned like candles. The Haida also paddled canoes to wage war and forge marriage alliances and to invite people to feasts and potlatches. The guests arrived by canoe.

The classic canoe was streamlined, with upswept ends and a flared bow and stern. Most were painted, with a black hull and elaborate designs on the bow and stern, symbolizing supernatural beings. Virtually all the neighboring people of the Northwest Coast respected the skill of Haida craftsmen and the quality of their canoes. War canoes had the same sharp projecting prow as freight canoes. However, in addition to a two-dimensional painted design on the hull, they often had separate carved crests on the bow or stern. The high prows of large war canoes were often emblazoned with the crests of the owners. None of these full-sized canoes, known as head canoes, has survived.

The Haida learned how to rig sails from visiting sailors and sea captains. By the end of the eighteenth century, they had begun to fit most large canoes with two or three masts and sails of canvas or cedar bark mats. These faster craft were easier to handle in the water and could carry up to ten tons of cargo. This new craft probably led to the disappearance of the so-called head canoes. With their huge prows, they were perfect for the crests of war chiefs, but made the craft difficult to handle under sail.

Head canoes had almost disappeared by the middle of the nineteenth century. These canoes are known today only through drawings made by early European visitors to the coastal home of the Haida. In fact, over the past hundred years, the knowledge of canoemaking has nearly been lost, although attempts have been made to revive the art. Several canoes have been built in the last decade. One of the finest examples of a war canoe was made by Alfred Davidson with the help of other master canoemakers. The canoe's paintings were designed and rendered by Charles Edenshaw.

In 1985, Bill Reid was commissioned to make a fifty-foot dugout canoe for Expo 86, the World's Fair in Vancouver, British Columbia. He named this lovely craft *Lootaas*, or Wave Eater. After the fair, several fiberglass replicas were made, of which the first two were for the Canadian Museum of Civilization. Taken to France, the original canoe was paddled up the Seine River to Paris in honor of the bicentennial of the French Revolution. Later, it sailed from Vancouver to Haida Gwaii and is now kept at Skidegate for special ceremonies.

## Warfare

The Haida viewed warfare as a ceremonial act. They were renowned for their practice of making quick surprise attacks upon their enemies. Their expertise as seamen, their superior canoes, and their protection from retaliation in their isolated archipelago made them greatly feared along the Northwest Coast.

Warriors protected themselves with armor, including round war helmets, bentwood visors, and wooden-slat breastplates, which were often worn beneath leather tunics emblazoned with their crests. Only a few Haida breastplates have survived, although numerous Tlingit examples may now be found in museums. Body armor included a war coat, made of the tough hides of sea lions or several layers of elk skin.

The Haida traded on the Nass River for the elk skins and acquired sea lion hides from European and American traders who had traded for them from native peoples at the mouth of the Columbia River.

For countless generations, the Haida relied on bows and arrows along with short spears and daggers for combat. However, as soon as firearms became available early in the nineteenth century, they adopted the new weaponry. Some owners even carved their crests onto the stocks of their muskets. War daggers, however, continued to be favored in hand-to-hand combat, and their use developed into an art form.

Hollowed out of a single cedar tree and manned by fifty to sixty warriors, large war canoes swept up and down the coast from Sitka in the north to the delta of the Fraser River in the south. Each canoe usually carried a medicine man to capture and annihilate the souls of enemies before battle. Women occasionally accompanied the warriors and fought as ably as the men.

The Haida often went to war to seize highly valued shieldlike copper plates and Chilkat blankets, which were scarce on the islands, as well as slaves. These captives worked in the villages or were traded to other native peoples. High-ranking people were also kidnapped from other tribes and then ransomed for objects of wealth. The anthropologist John R. Swanton found a link between warfare and potlatching among the Haida. He stated, "Feasts . . . and the potlatches were the Haida roads to greatness more than war. The latter, when not waged to avenge injuries, was simply a means of increasing their power to give the former."

Even in ancient times, the Haida engaged in sea battles. They tied cedar bark ropes to heavy stone rings and hurled them at enemy canoes. Weighing forty to fifty pounds, the stones could shatter the side of a canoe, causing it to capsize. Most native peoples avoided sea battles with the Haida, trying instead to draw them ashore for combat. The Tsimshian lit signal fires to warn their villages on the Skeena River when Haida invaders approached the mainland.

Fortified sites were part of the defensive strategy of all Northwest Coast people, including the Haida, for at least two thousand years. Captain James Cook was so impressed with one Haida fort off the west coast of Graham Island that he called it Hippah Island after the Maori forts he had seen in New Zealand. Military defenses at these forts included palisades, rolling top-log defenses, heavy trapdoors, and fighting platforms stocked with boulders to throw at attackers.

The intensity of warfare increased between 1780 and 1830. During this time, the Haida subdued all their enemies except the growing number of European and American traders arriving on their shores. The Haida captured more than half a dozen ships, including the *Eleanora*, which was taken by chiefs of the village of Skungwai (or Ninstints) because Chief Koyah had been mistreated by the captain of this ship. Even more dramatic was the capture of the ship *Susan Sturgis* by Chief Wiah of Masset and the later rescue of the crew by Albert Edward Edenshaw.

In these and other conflicts, the Haida quickly learned the fighting tactics of their adversaries, including the use of cannons. As early as 1795, a British trading ship fired its cannons at a village in the central part of Haida Gwaii after several of its crew members had been killed by the inhabitants. However, the British had to flee when the Haida shot back at them with their own cannon. They found out later that the Haida had taken a cannon and ammunition from an American schooner. The Haida also mounted swivel guns on many of their war canoes, although the recoil on discharge split the hulls of many craft. By the 1830s, warfare, which had become too costly for fur traders on the Northwest Coast, gave way to a peace known as the Pax Britannica.

# 4.Beliefs

Mortuary poles, such as this double pole carved by Bill Reid and Doug Cranmer, were erected to honor the dead.

THE HAIDA BELIEVED IN A GREAT SPIRIT WHOM THEY CALLED NE-KILST-LASS. This spirit assumed the form of the Raven known as Choo-e-ah. Ne-kilst-lass created the world, drawing light and order from black chaos. He organized the system of clans and gave the people their ceremonies, language, and culture, along with many useful things. Yet he could also be imperfect, even contradictory, bringing evil and confusion to the people.

The Haida have long held animals in high regard. They not only believed that spirits dwelt in all living creatures, but that animals were more intelligent than humans. One of the most important rituals was held to thank the salmon for returning to the stream each year and providing life-giving food for the people. Animals were thought to be kind enough to allow themselves to be killed and eaten to sustain the people.

The Haida and other coastal peoples shared many beliefs about the blending of the natural and spiritual worlds. Common beliefs had to do with curing the sick, ensuring a good harvest of fish and game, and influencing the weather. Known as *Haida Sah-gah*, shamans, or medicine men, enjoyed special powers in vital tasks, such as trading expeditions and warfare. They were also referred to as skaggy, a shortened version of the Haida words for "long-haired one," because they wore their hair long and tied atop their heads. Women could be shaman, but more often men accepted the calling. Women usually specialized in curing sickness and assisting at childbirth. Some also had power over animals and fish. Shaman came from any rank except slaves, but most often belonged to high-ranking families. Many had a brother who was a chief. In this way, the family maintained both spiritual and political power within their lineage.

Medicine men healed both the body and the spirit. They usually inherited this calling, which came down from maternal uncle to nephew. There were no special stages or degrees that led to becoming a shaman. A young man was instructed by another shaman, usually his uncle, and would become a shaman as soon as he learned the system of beliefs.

Yet to become a shaman, a person had to be possessed, or overcome, by a supernatural being, or *sga'na*, and so chosen as a medium. Falling into a trance or coma, the person experienced death and rebirth. Through the shaman, the spirit could then influence the human world. When the spirit was present, the shaman's own identity was almost completely lost—he became the spirit itself. The shaman dressed as the spirit instructed him and spoke in the spirit's language. Before he died, a shaman revealed the secret of possession to his successor, who might begin with a weaker spirit and, over time, acquire spirits with greater strength.

The main classes of supernatural beings were the Canoe-People, the Forest-People, and the Above-People. Drawing power from the spirit world, shamans foretold the future, healed the sick, brought good fortune to hunting or fishing expeditions, and influenced the weather. They guided the people in the mysteries of birth and death and in the relations between animals and humans and between nature and the spirit world. Because of their contact with feared spirits, however, shamans had to live outside the village.

Shamans relied on beautifully crafted sacred objects. Small figures—miniature masks attached to headdresses and sewn on aprons—represented their spirit helpers. Shamans were guided by visions, which were revealed to them in songs and through amulets. Weak from fasting or illness, they often slipped into trances, during which they called on spirits to ward off disease, evil spirits, and the spells of other shamans or witches. Sacred figures also guarded the body of a deceased shaman, which was often placed in a small mortuary house along the shore.

*The Haida decorated tools and other objects, such as this ceremonial drum, which became lovely to the eye as well as the ear.*

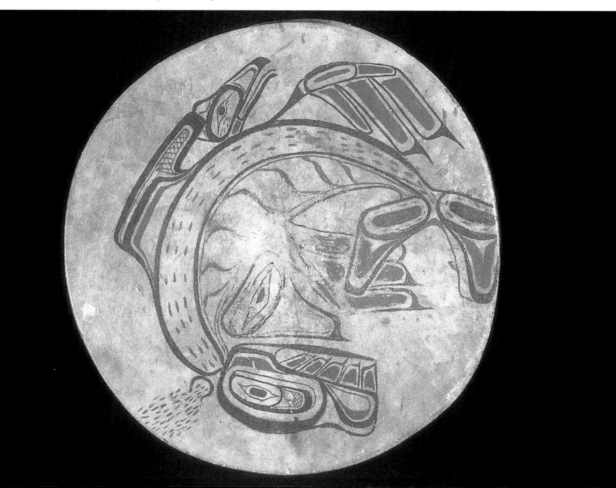

The shaman also used "soul catchers," carved bone tubes with wooden stoppers, to help sick people whose souls had departed from the body. He chanted and invoked spells until the soul was ensnared in the soul catcher. He then returned the soul to the ill person in hopes of bringing recovery. During curing ceremonies, the shaman wore a crown of bear claws, goat horns, wood and bone. He approached the sick, holding a rattle to both announce his arrival and drive away evil. He knocked on the floor and poked the ill person, urging him, "Get up, get up." If the person was not able to do so, the skaggy attempted other cures. He might practice more conventional medicine, such as lancing an infected wound with a sharply pointed bone, or he might call upon the spirits to drive away evil forces.

Shamans were occasionally feared as witches. It was believed they could steal one's soul and bring sickness upon a person. They also wielded great influence with the chief. They enjoyed wealth, social status, and power with the upper classes, charging fees according to the affluence of the patient's family. They could refuse to care for a patient, but if so, they might be blamed for the illness.

## Ceremonies

The Haida often held ceremonies during rainy weather, from November until March. These were both social and religious events. By the mid-1700s, the Haida had begun to hold secret society winter dances. While chiefs wielded political power, the Haida formed secret societies for dances and other ceremonies. They learned about secret societies and rituals from captives, especially those taken in war against the Heiltsuk. Since many of these captives were of low rank and did not fully understand their own secret societies, the knowledge they passed on was incomplete. Edward Curtis, who photographed many coastal peoples, observed that the Haida knew little of the myths on which the winter dances were based, although they used the names and performed the dances to honor the raising of a totem pole or the building of a house.

During secret society ceremonies people shook rattles, pounded drums, or blew whistles to draw forth the spirits of the forest and to renew their relationship with the supernatural. The spirits were thought to have inhabited the earth long before the coming of people. The Haida often sought the help of these spirits in their daily lives. The most powerful were those of the sky. With the first winter storms the spirits were thought to rise from a period of fasting and seek the haunts of the Haida. Through the long rainy winters, people brightened their days with feasts and rituals and with the creation of works of art.

Purification rituals were held before these ceremonies to prepare for the approach of the spirits. Participants dressed as befit their social position. During the dancing and singing, people relied on guardian figures for protection from disease, evil spirits, and the spells of shamans and witches. They wore charms representing helpful spirits on pendants or sewed them into their capes. Secret society members wore painted masks decorated with copper, abalone shell, and fur to make a beard and hairline. They also painted their faces and occasionally attached pieces of copper and abalone shell to their faces with glue made from halibut. They donned Chilkat blankets or cloaks with streamers of human hair and ornaments, such as the wooden dorsal fin of a killer whale, and carried a dancing spear, often decorated with spire designs.

The masks of secret society dancers symbolized the wild spirits of the forest, which were known as *gagiid*. The spirits had a thin, wrinkled face and a scowling mouth. Often a blue-green color, they portrayed a person close to drowning, whose skin had become cold

*These four Haida men were photographed at Masset between 1875 and 1885 in full ceremonial regalia.*

from the icy water. Like the Tsimshian, the Haida wore masks during potlatches to represent the spirit beings of their ancestors. After the 1840s, masks and argillite carvings were eagerly sought by seamen, traders and tourists, and the Haida began to make these articles not for traditional ceremonies, but as souvenirs. Of the several thousand masks held in private and museum collections, it is hard to determine which were made for actual use rather than for sale.

Spirit dances were held as a coming-of-age ritual for both girls and boys. The young person first wandered through the forests for several days, hoping to find a guiding spirit. Or the young person might be symbolically kidnaped by an animal spirit that took the child into the forest and then returned his or her supposedly dead body. The most powerful spirit that a person could receive was the Eagle or Raven—though women usually obtained their power from birds such as Woodpecker or Snipe. The spirit made its presence known through a song revealed in a vision. The song was taught to the tribal leaders, who then sang it during the dance.

Young people spent eleven days behind a curtain—supposedly dead for eight days and in the hands of the spirits for the other three. On the twelfth morning the initiates appeared on the beach as if they were wild creatures just emerged from the forest. The members of the society caught them with ropes and dragged them into a house. In the evening all the people gathered to exorcize the spirit that possessed the initiates. Led through the front door by their attendants, the initiates then danced round the fire and withdrew behind a curtain. When they reappeared, they danced in various costumes until they were "tamed." Spirit dancers attired themselves in dress that symbolized how the spirit had appeared to them. They might wear a mask or a shredded bark headdress from which hung streamers or shells. Some dancers painted their faces and bodies in red or black. Participants danced through the night and did sleight-of-hand tricks, such as seemingly decapitating an initiate and then restoring his or her life.

Potlatches and secret society ceremonies were among the most important rituals in Haida society. However, secret societies and winter dances began to disappear when missionaries arrived in the mid-1870s, although they were held occasionally for another decade. One of the last dances was held at Skidegate in the 1880s. Yet in the early 1900s, Edward Curtis found people who clearly remembered the events from their childhood. Traditional ceremonies were out-lawed for a time, but the repeal of these laws has led to the creation of modern versions of ancient rituals, along with the renewal of tra-ditional arts.

## Stories

Stories recounted mythical encounters with spirits, many of which were animals. The Haida had great respect for animals and considered it wrong not to aid them in distress. If a person failed to do so, he or she had to leave the community. The beliefs of the Haida, like other coastal tribes, were based on an epic cycle of stories about the Raven and his many exploits. After bringing forth the first humans from a clamshell, the Raven established order in the uni-

*Stories often related the living link between the people and the land.*

verse, only to threaten this balance with utter chaos later on. Greedy and mischievous, the Raven almost inadvertently instructed people in the art of living. In one of the best-known stories, the Raven disguised himself and entered the house of the Sky Chief, from whom he stole the sun, moon, and stars to present as a gift to the people. In another well-known story, the Raven was hungry and decided to swim underwater to steal the bait from the hooks of some halibut fishermen. However, the hook stuck tightly in his beak. The fishermen banded together to haul in what they thought was a huge halibut, only to find the Raven's beak. Many stories recount how the Raven acquired useful things for humans from supernatural beings, such as fresh water, salmon, the fish weir, and the house. Here is one such story about the Raven:

## "The Girl Who Fed a Raven"

One day a girl's father returned from fishing on the ocean. Her mother cut up the fish he had caught. The girl took the liver and fat of the halibut and gave it to a raven. She continued to feed the Raven until spring arrived, although her family and others in the village had little food.

One day the Raven flew down in front of the girl. He made eating motions and beckoned her to follow him. She did so, and he showed her a large pile of mollusks and other delicious shellfish on the sand at the edge of the sea. The girl brought the shellfish to her uncles' wives who were grateful for the food. The next day the girl returned to the beach at low tide where she again gathered sea creatures along the shore. She brought the shellfish back and gave them to others in the village.

Because the girl had fed him, the Raven continued to help her. One day, she found the tail of a salmon. She took home the scrap, and miraculously it grew into a whole spring salmon. She found a porpoise tail and the same thing happened.

Another time, as she was looking for food at low tide, two men approached her. They took her to the chief of their village, and she was held captive in his house. After she had stayed there a long while, the Raven flew into the village to help her. He told the people, "I cut up a black whale that floated ashore at North Cape."

The people somehow knew that she had brought the Raven to them. The chief said, "Give the woman food in exchange for the help she has given us."

The people eagerly gave her an abundance of food—halibut tails and heads and berries—and she was allowed to go home. She had been gone for a long time, and her father did not know where to look for her. However, the next morning, she was sitting in front of her father's house surrounded by huge piles of food. She gave some of the food to her uncles' wives and traded the rest for goods. She then gave these trade goods to her father, and he became a rich man.

Afterward, she told her father what the Raven had said about the black whale. "You should look for the whale at the point of North Cape," she said.

*T*his detail from a totem pole tells a story about a way of life that was nearly lost.

He went there and found the whale. The huge creature had not been touched by the people of the other village. He cut up a portion of the blubber and then returned to the village and told the people about the beached whale. Everyone joyfully rushed to the beach and helped to cut up the whale, which would provide them with food.

For a long time, people had plenty of food and they were grateful—to the girl and to the Raven.

## Games and Gambling

The Haida enjoyed several popular games that included a bit of lively gambling. One, similar to pick-up sticks, was played with slender decorated sticks that are now so highly sought by collectors that none have been preserved in museums.

Another game relied on three sets of sticks, each named after a different animal or bird, known only to the owner and his family. Made from hard maple, the sticks were carved, painted, and engraved with a hot poker. Talented artists burned the designs and inlaid many sticks with abalone shell or copper. The most elaborate sticks are vivid examples of Haida art—many include fifty or more drawings. The complex illustrations wrapped around the sticks, which had to be rotated slowly for the complete effect. For example, shaman figures seemed to jump as in an animated cartoon when the stick was turned. In others, birds seemed to fly and killer whales leap around the stick. Tiny complex scenes that documented the Haida way of life, such as war parties venturing forth in canoes, men hunting sea otters, and fishermen bringing in their catch, were also popular.

Gambling sticks were used on a special leather mat often decorated with painted or engraved images of crests. It was believed that the crest brought good luck to those who then inherited them. For safekeeping, a set of Haida gambling sticks might be kept in a painted deerskin bag.

# 5. Changing World

This painting depicts the Santiago—the first European ship to reach Haida Gwaii. Under Captain Juan Pérez, the ship sailed past in 1774.

It is believed that the first European ship to reach the Queen Charlotte Islands was the *Santiago*, under Captain Juan Pérez, which sailed past in 1774. Pérez was sent to investigate the activity of the Russians in Alaska. Though a French ship later passed by on a similar mission, it was not until 1787 that the Haida directly encountered Europeans. A British sea captain arrived, naming the islands after his ship, the *Queen Charlotte*, and began to trade with the Haida. The British wanted furs, especially the pelts of sea otters, which were in great demand in China, and the Haida desired iron tools with which they could carve more elaborate totems, canoes, and houses. Since the Haida were experienced traders, the Europeans were not able to take advantage of them. Initially, these outsiders did not attempt to change the traditional Haida way of life.

With their new tools, the Haida reached new artistic heights in woodcarving. Yet their interactions with Europeans soon devastated them. The sea otter nearly went extinct from overtrapping, and diseases brought by the Europeans soon infected the Haida. In 1774, between fifteen and thirty thousand people may have lived on Haida Gwaii in at least fifty thriving villages. After several smallpox epidemics ravaged the villages, the most deadly in 1862, about 95 percent of the Haida population was wiped out. A census undertaken by the Hudson's Bay Company in 1885 counted only 800 Haida. By 1915, the population had fallen to just 588 people, leaving the Haida at the brink of extinction.

Arriving in the late 1800s, missionaries preached that totem poles were false idols and that potlatches were evil customs. Totem poles

*B*arely one hundred years after the Haida first encountered Europeans, there were many abandoned villages on Haida Gwaii.

were destroyed, and in 1884, the Canadian government outlawed potlatches, which were held in secret until the law was reversed in recent years. By the turn of the century, Methodist missionaries had taken control of the education of Haida children and actively discouraged traditional culture. Not until the 1970s, due to the efforts of artist Bill Reid, was a totem pole again erected on the Queen Charlotte Islands.

Until 1867, the Haida of Alaska lived on land claimed by Russia. This nation had little effect on Haida culture beyond converting a few people to the Russian Orthodox Church. However, Russia then sold the territory to the United States. Miners and settlers poured into Alaska during the gold rush of the late 1800s, and doomed the Haida way of life. Many Haida became fishermen and loggers for American companies. When the community of Hydaburg was established, attempts were made to educate and "civilize" the native peoples, including the Haida. In 1911, a Presbyterian mission was founded near Haida villages. Three of the villages were abandoned when the government failed to support them. The people moved reluctantly into the town of Hydaburg, where they formed the last organized Haida community in Alaska.

## Language

Haida is not related to any of the forty-five native languages spoken in the Pacific Northwest. It has been likened to the rhythmic sound of waves on the shores and the cries of birds hovering overhead. However, the language has nearly been extinguished. Children no longer speak the language of their parents and grandparents, although they may be familiar with traditional Haida songs. Today, two dialects from the language survive at Skidegate and Masset in the Queen Charlotte Islands. The Masset dialect is also spoken by the Haida who migrated to Alaska in the 1700s. Efforts are now being made to revive the culture and the musical language of these coastal people.

Here are some examples of the dialect of the Haida of Alaska based on the *Haida Dictionary* compiled by Erma Lawrence. Some letters are pronounced as in English, but others have no English equivalent. These simplified examples will give you an idea of how to pronounce some Haida words.

The vowels are pronounced as follows:

| | |
|---|---|
| a | as in s*u*n |
| aa | as in f*a*ther, |
| ei | as in d*ay* |
| i | as in p*i*n |
| ii | as in b*ea*n |
| o | as in l*ow* |
| u | as in p*u*t |
| uu | as in m*oo*n |

| | |
|---|---|
| beach | chaaw salii |
| black bear | taan |
| canoe | tluu |
| clam | kyuu |
| dance | xyaahl |
| dog | xa |
| drum | gawjaaw |
| eagle | guut |
| father | hadaa |
| fire | tsaanuu |
| girl | jaadaa |

| | |
|---|---|
| halibut | xakw |
| house | na |
| island | gwaay |
| kelp | hlkaam |
| king crab | huugaa |
| king salmon | taawun |
| land | tlak |
| moon | kung |
| mother | aw |
| night | sancyaa |
| no | geih |
| ocean | siigaay |
| oyster | tluxtlux |
| rain | dal |
| raven | yaahl |
| razor clams | kamahl |
| red cedar | tsuu |
| river | gantl |
| rock | kwaa |
| sand | taas |
| seal | xuut |
| stormy | gatuwaa |
| tree | kiit |
| village | laanaa |
| water | gantl |
| wind | tajaaw |
| yes | aang |

# Renaissance of Haida Art

A golden age of Haida art began in the 1850s and flourished for half a century. During this time native artists found ready markets among tourists in Victoria and along the Northwest Coast for replicas of massive traditional works. A great number of skilled artists also burst forth with innovative objects based on their rich heritage.

It was not considered acceptable to sign one's name to a piece of art. Instead, artists created subtle variations in style. The best-known artists of the golden age include Albert Edward Edenshaw, John Robson, John Cross, and Charles Edenshaw, along with carver Tom Price and Masset artist Simeon Stiltla. The golden age ended as lineage groups broke apart into separate families that did not continue traditions.

When the last two artists of the period died—Charles Edenshaw in 1920 and John Cross in 1939—Rufus Moody and several other artists kept alive the creative spirit of Haida art. Then another generation of fine artists, many of whom had studied in art schools, rekindled the flame, leading in the 1950s to a renaissance of Haida art. Artists such as Bill Reid, Robert Davidson, and Jim Hart flourished despite the near extinction of their people.

Today Haida art is admired around the world for its monumental totem poles and sculptures and its fine carving in wood, metal, and slate. Over the generations, artists have refined a distinctive style, which they apply to both sculpture and two-dimensional works. The ocean and its creatures—killer whales, sea lions, halibut, sharks, and supernatural beings such as the sea-wolf—remain sources of inspiration.

*H*ere are several examples of Haida art: an ivory totem, a gold brooch, as well as a dish and panel made of argillite.

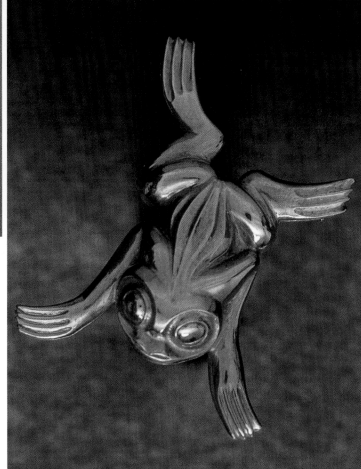

# 6. The Haida Today

The Haida have struggled to preserve their homeland and keep the countless acres intact.

AFTER THE SMALLPOX EPIDEMICS, THE SURVIVORS MOVED TO TWO CENTRAL villages on the islands—Skidegate at the south end of Graham Island, and Old Masset in the north at the mouth of Masset Inlet. Today, these two villages are growing rapidly. Although the economy of the islands has been based on the forest industry and commercial fisheries since the 1930s, declining fish stocks and forest resources are prompting new approaches to making a living. Tourism and wood manufacturing, as well as arts and crafts, are among the most important economic mainstays on the islands today.

Old Masset and Skidegate are each governed by a village council. The Council of the Haida Nation has also been formed to work with the two village councils and with clans and individuals in addressing broad political concerns. The Council of the Haida Nation is especially concerned with asserting titles to land and protecting the rights of the people. The council is currently negotiating a treaty and land claims agreement with the Canadian government and the province of British Columbia.

Over the course of the twentieth century, the Haida population has recovered somewhat. But even today there are only about 1,600 people in the villages of Masset and Skidegate and another 1,800 people living in the United States—including those in Hydaburg, Alaska, a small city on the south end of Prince of Wales Island. Others have scattered to find work in larger cities, such as Kasaan and Ketchikan, Alaska, and Seattle, Washington. As the Haida seek their rights to land and resources in Alaska it is believed that they will enjoy a resurgence in traditional culture.

**A**lthough they have adopted Western styles of dress, children continue to uphold many of the traditions of their ancestors.

Many Haida in Alaska and on the Queen Charlotte Islands now earn a living through logging, although some others disapproved. The Haida on the Queen Charlotte Islands have been engaged in nonviolent protests against logging on their sacred tribal lands. In 1985, Haida leaders were arrested, charged with contempt of court, and imprisoned after they blocked a logging road for several months. In 1987, the Canadian government established a national park on South Moresby, the location of one of the few first-growth coastal rain forests left in the world. Although the creation of Gwaii Hanaas National Park preserves the forest, other lands are still being clear-cut, and many people believe that all tribal lands should be returned to the Haida.

Other Haida support themselves by fishing, which has also had its difficulties. In 1994, Canadian officials started to lower the limits on catches, and two years later they banned chinook salmon fishing altogether. The chinook salmon, known as the king salmon in Alaska, has suffered from many years of overfishing. The decline has hurt the economies of many towns on the Pacific coast, especially Masset, where many people have lost their jobs in fish processing operations.

On the Queen Charlotte Islands, many Haida offer tourist services, and some people have achieved international acclaim as painters and carvers of traditional artworks. The village of Sgan Gwaii, on Anthony Island, abandoned since a smallpox epidemic in the 1860s, now has a totem pole restoration project underway. Archaeologists have been studying Sgan Gwaii, an official UNESCO World Heritage Site and a Canadian national park preserve. Objects discovered there must now be returned to the Haida people and housed in the Queen Charlotte Islands Museum.

Incredibly, Haida culture has survived. Today, the population has grown to around 3,500 people. There are still two main groups of Haida who live in scattered villages in British Columbia and Alaska. The two bands joined forces in 1980 to form the Council of the Haida Nation. Although they also take part in mainstream Western culture, the Haida remain dedicated to passing on their language, customs, and art forms to future generations.

More About

the Haida

# Time Line

**about 1000 B.C.** Ancestors of the Haida settle on the Queen Charlotte Islands

**1774** First contact with Europeans when a Spanish ship arrives at the Queen Charlotte Islands

**1787** The Haida begin to trade with the British, who name the Queen Charlotte Islands

**1791** First smallpox epidemic sweeps through Haida villages

**1867** United States purchases Alaska from Russia

**1871** Canada enacts the Indian Act that defines the relationship between native peoples and the government

**1882** The Haida and representatives of the province of British Columbia agree to boundaries for 37 reserves, totaling nearly three-and-a-half million acres

**1884** Canadian government outlaws potlatches and ceremonial dances

**1912** President William H. Taft establishes a small reservation—barely twelve acres—for the Haida

**1926** President Calvin Coolidge abolishes the reservation and establishes a two-acre school reserve

**1936** The Haida of Alaska form the town of Hydaburg and adopt a constitution under the Indian Reorganization Act—the first native Alaskan group to do so

**1952** The Haida of Hydaburg and the Tlingits petition the federal government for a reservation of 900,000 acres

**1968** The Alaska Haida along with the Tlingit are awarded seven-and-a-half million dollars from the U. S. Court of Claims as compensation for land taken from them

**1971** The U. S. Congress passes the Alaska Native Claims Settlement Act. The Haida of Hydaburg join the Sealaska Corporation and the Haida Corporation

**1985** Seventy-two Haida and their supporters are arrested as they attempt to stop logging operations on the Queen Charlotte Islands

**1987** Canadian officials sign a Memorandum of Understanding, which creates a national park and national marine park in the Queen Charlotte Islands

# Notable People

**Eda'nsa** (about 1810–1894), a Haida chief who also called himself Captain Douglas, was born on Graham Island, one of the Queen Charlotte Islands. In 1841, Eda'nsa, whose name means Melting Ice from a Glacier, became Eagle chief of the Sta Stas Shongalth lineage, one of three groups that vied for leadership of the Eagle town of Kiusta on Graham Island. When he became chief, Eda'nsa succeeded in taking charge of the town, and throughout his life he endeavored to be the greatest Haida leader of all time. Eda'nsa became a trader in native slaves, which he acquired by bartering with or raiding other native peoples. He also served as a guide for white traders through the waters of the Queen Charlotte Islands. Eda'nsa became a Christian in 1884 and continued his work as a trader until his death. He was succeeded by his nephew Charlie Edenshaw, a highly regarded Haida artist.

**Charles Edenshaw** (1839–1924), wood carver and silversmith, was raised at Skidegate on Graham Island, the largest of the Queen Charlotte Islands. When his father died, Charles moved to Masset with his mother. He became skilled as a carver of wood and argillite, as well as a fine silversmith. Highly regarded as an artist, he achieved great wealth by trading his art with other tribes and visitors. When his uncle Albert, a Haida chief, died, Edenshaw was selected to replace him because of his heritage, great wealth, and artistic skill. He lived in the Haida village of Yatza, where he and his wife raised their five children. During the late 1800s and early 1900s, scholars such as John Swanton and Franz Boas consulted Edenshaw about Haida culture. Edenshaw made sketches and model totems and provided information on Haida symbols and mythology.

**Bill Reid** (1920–1998), a distinguished artist, was born in Victoria, British Columbia. In his early years he was unaware of his Haida ancestry, but he later became the most important figure in the late twentieth-century renaissance of Haida art. Reid's background was cross-cultural. His father, William, an American of Scottish-German descent, followed the newly built railroad into northern British Columbia, where he ran a hotel in Smithers. Reid's mother, Sophie, was a Haida with an Anglican education that led her to conceal her heritage from her son.

Shortly after William and Sophie married, he moved his hotel business to Hyder, B.C., on the Alaska border while she set up house in Victoria, B.C., and made a living as a dressmaker, designing fashionable clothes for wealthy families of the city. For a number of years the family moved back and forth between the two locations, and Reid received his education in a variety of schools. When he was twelve years old he made his first crafts— carving miniature shapes out of blackboard chalk, including a totem pole and a Viking boat. He did not learn of his Haida heritage until his teens. However, the gold and silver jewelry with Haida designs that his aunts wore when they visited his mother introduced him to the art of his ancestors.

Years later, at age twenty-three, he visited his mother's home village of Skidegate and met her father, Charles Gladstone, and other older members of the community who still had knowledge of Haida traditions. Reid learned that his grandfather had been a carver of argillite and an engraver of silver bracelets. Gladstone had probably learned these skills from his uncle, the great nineteenth-century Haida sculptor Charles Edenshaw, whose tools he inherited, and whom Reid subsequently adopted as his hero. Reid's life as an artist reflected not only his ethnic background but also the particular tradition of his mother's family.

During his education, he acquired a taste for romantic literature, poetry, and classical music, but had no formal training in art. After finishing high school, he became a radio announcer for local stations in eastern Canada and eventually joined the Canadian Broadcasting Corporation in Toronto in 1948. A modest and unassuming man, he was never entirely comfortable with broadcasting. In Toronto he was further exposed to Haida heritage through the Northwest Coast collection in the Royal Ontario Museum, especially a totem pole from Tanu, the village where his grandmother was born into the Raven moiety. Later that year, he decided to try to follow in his grandfather's footsteps and enrolled in a jewelry-making course at the Ryerson Institute of Technology. After finishing the course, he undertook an apprenticeship at the Platinum Art Company in Toronto.

Returning to Vancouver in 1951, he set up a basement workshop for making jewelry between his working hours at the CBC. He applied the European jewelry-making techniques he had learned to Haida designs. It was at this time that he began to focus on the works of Edenshaw, which he first encountered in the form of two gold bracelets at his grandfather's funeral in 1954. He studied the several hundred pieces of gold and silver jewelry by Edenshaw in museums and copied images collected by John R. Swanton, Franz Boas, Marius Barbeau, and other scholars of Haida myths and argillite carvings.

Reid became involved with totem pole salvage and restoration projects of the Royal British Columbia Museum and the University of British Columbia's department of anthropology. Through the museum he gained his first professional wood carving experience during a brief stint working with Kwakwaka'wakw (Kwakiutl) master carver Mungo Martin. Then, in 1958, after reading on-air an item about a UBC department of anthropology project to reconstruct a section of a Haida village, he promptly applied for the job and resigned from the CBC. He spent the following years teaching himself the craft of pole-making. These poles, which were completed in 1962, are now outdoor exhibits at the UBC Museum of Anthropology.

Reid is credited with initiating a renaissance in Haida art in the 1950s. There is now, thanks to him, an international demand for carvings, totems, jewelry, and baskets. His own sculptures stand outside the British Columbia Museum of Anthropology, the Vancouver Aquarium, and the Canadian Embassy in Washington. For over twenty-five years before his

*Bill Reid*

death, Reid struggled with Parkinson's disease. Sometimes he had only a few hours, or even minutes, of productive time in which he could sculpt. However, his mind and determination remained strong, and he was able to proceed with his projects thanks to willing helpers, who would put aside their own artistic endeavors to help with Reid's projects.

He received honorary doctorates from Simon Fraser University, the University of Victoria, York University, the University of Western Ontario, Trent University, the University of British Columbia, and the University of Toronto. His awards include the Canada Council's Molson Prize for cultural achievement (1976), and one of Canada's highest tokens of recognition in this field, the Diplôme d'Honneur (Canadian Conference of the Arts) for Service to the Arts (1979). In 1994, he received the Canadian National Aboriginal Achievement Award.

The most renowned Haida artist of the twentieth century, Reid has also published *The Raven Steals the Light*, which recounts an important Haida story. Upon his death, David Silcox wrote in the *Toronto Globe and Mail*, "He never lost his sense of being a servant of a great tradition."

# Glossary

**commoner**  One of the classes of people in Haida society who did not own houses and other valuable property.

**crest figure**  A bird, fish, or other animal that symbolizes one's lineage, often painted or carved on homes, totem poles, and other personal property.

**Haida Gwaii**  The Haida name for the Queen Charlotte Islands.

**head canoe**  A war canoe with a high prow, often emblazoned with the crest of its owner.

**lineage**  A group of people descended from a common ancestor.

**matrilineal**  Tracing descent through the mother's side of the family.

**noble**  The wealthy and respected upper class of the Haida, who owned houses and considerable property.

**potlatch**  A lavish ceremonial feast held on special occasions in which the host gives away many valuable presents.

**reserve**  Land set aside by the Canadian or United State governments for an Indian tribe; called a reservation in the United States.

**skaggy**  A medicine man or shaman.

**totem pole**  Carved wooden poles on which people displayed their crests and related family histories.

# Further Information

There are many excellent resources available for learning more about native peoples. The following books and websites were consulted in researching and writing *The Haida*:

Barbeau, C. Marius. *Totem Poles, Vol.1 and 2*. Anthropological Series 30, *National Museum of Canada Bulletin 119,*1950.

Curtis, Edward. *The North American Indian, Vol.II, The Nootka, The Haida*. New York: Johnson Reprint Corp. 1970.

Dickson, Olive Patricia. *Canada's First Nations*. Norman: University of Oklahoma Press, 1992.

Dawson, George Mercer. *The Haidas*. Third Edition of Facsimile. Seattle, Wash.: Shorey Book Store, 1967.

Drew, Leslie. *Haida: Their Art and Culture*. Surrey, B.C.; Blaine, Wash.: Hancock House, 1982.

Enrico, John James. *Northern Haida Songs*. Lincoln: University of Nebraska Press, 1996.

Enrico, John, ed. *Skidegate Haida Myths and Histories*. Skidegate, B.C.: Queen Charlotte Islands Museum Press, 1995.

Hodge, F. W. *Handbook of Indians of Canada*. New York: Kraus Reprint Co., 1969.

Jonaitis, Aldona. *From the Land of the Totem Poles*. Seattle: University of Washington Press, 1988.

MacDonald, George F. *Chiefs of the Sea and Sky: Haida Heritage Sites of the Queen Charlotte Islands*. Vancouver: University of British Columbia Press, 1993.

MacDonald, George F. *Haida Art*. Hull: Canadian Museum of Civilization, and Vancouver, B.C.: Douglas and McIntyre, 1996.

MacDonald, George F. *Haida Monumental Art: Villages of the Queen Charlotte Islands*. Vancouver: University of British Columbia Press, 1993.

Reid, William. *The Raven Steals the Light*. Vancouver, B.C.: Douglas & McIntyre; Seattle: University of Washington Press, 1984.

Shadbolt, Doris. *Bill Reid*. Vancouver, B.C.: Douglas and McIntyre; Seattle: University of Washington Press, 1986.

Steltzer, Ulli. *A Haida Potlatch*. Vancouver, B.C.: Douglas & McIntyre, 1984.

Swanton, John R. *Contributions to the Ethnology of the Haida*. Publications of the Jesup North Pacific Expedition 5(1); American Museum of Natural History Memoirs 8(1). Leiden, The Netherlands: E.J. Brill; New York: G.E. Stechert, 1905.

Swanton, John R. *Haida Texts and Myths: Skidegate Dialect*. Bureau of American Ethnology Bulletin 29. Washington, D.C.: Government Printing Office, 1905.

Young people who wish to learn more about the Haida will enjoy these excellent books for children:

Adams, Dawn. *Haida Art*. Vancouver, B.C.: Wedge, 1983.

Bonvillain, Nancy. *The Haidas: People of the Northwest Coast*. Brookfield, Conn.: Millbrook Press, 1994.

Gridley, Marion Eleanor. *The Story of the Haida*. New York: Putnam, 1972.

Nelson, Jenny. *The Weavers*. Vancouver, B. C.: Pacific Educational Press, 1992.

Oliviero, Jamie. *The Day Sun Was Stolen*. Winnipeg: Hyperion Press, 1995.

Siska, Heather Smith. *The Haida and the Inuit People of the Seasons*. Vancouver, B.C.: Douglas & McIntyre (Educational), 1984.

"The First Haida" is adapted from stories first published in *Tales from the Totems of the Hidery*, Volume 2. Chicago: Archives of the International Folk-

Lore Association, 1899. "The Girl Who Fed a Raven" is adapted from Haida Texts and Myths: Skidegate Dialect, recorded by John R. Swanton and published by the Smithsonian Institution, Bureau of American Ethnology, *Bulletin 29.*


## *Organizations*

**CCTHITA (Central Council of the Tlingit and Haida Indian Tribes of Alaska)**
320 W. Willoughby Ave.
Suite 300
Juneau, AK 99801
Phone: 1-800-344-1432 or (907) 463-7100
Fax 907-586-8970

**Haida Nation, Council of the**
P.O. Box 589
Masset, B.C., Canada, V0T 1M0
Phone: 250-626-5252
Fax: 250-626-3403

**Old Masset Village Council**
P.O. Box 189
Old Massett BC V0T 1M0
Phone: 250-626-3337
Fax: 250-626-5440

**Skidegate**
Box 1301
Skidegate BC V0T 1S1
Phone: 250-559-4496
Fax: 250-559-8247

## Websites

**Alaska Native Knowledge Network**
http://www.ankn.uaf.edu/

**British Columbia Ministry of Aboriginal Affairs**
http://www.aaf.gov.bc.ca/aaf/

**Canadian Museum of Civilization**
http://www.civilization.ca/

**Central Council of the Tlingit and Haida Indian Tribes of Alaska**
http://www.tlingit-haida.org/

**Department of Indian Affairs and Northern Development**
http://www.inac.gc.ca/index_e.html

**First Peoples' Cultural Foundation**
http://www.ntc.bc.ca/

**Gwaii Haanas**
http://fas.sfu.ca/parkscan/gwaii/

**The Haida: Children of Eagle and Raven**
http://www.civilization.ca/membrs/fph/haida/haindexe.html

**Haida Gwaii Museum at Quay 'Ilnagaay**
http://www.museumsassn.bc.ca/~bcma/museums/qcim.html

**Haida: Spirits of the Sea**
http://www.chin.gc.ca/haida/nojava/english/home/index.html

**Maltwood Art Museum and Gallery**
http://www.maltwood.uvic.ca/~maltwood/

**Museum of Anthropology at the University of British Columbia**
http://www.moa.ubc.ca/

**Parks Canada**
http://parkscanada.pch.gc.ca

**Royal British Columbia Museum**
http://rbcm1.rbcm.gov.bc.ca/index_vi.html

**Tlingit & Haida Central Council**
http://www.tlingit-haida.org/frameright.html

**Woodland Cultural Centre**
http://www.ciphermedia.com/WOODLAND/MM.HTML

# Index

soul-catchers, 83
spirits, 67, 80–81, 82, 84–86
storage, 38
stories. *See* myths

taboos, 56
Tlingit, 12, 34, 68, 71
tools, 15, 28, 36, 38, 50–51, 59, 65, 82, **82**,
    92–93, 96
totem poles, 15, **26–27**, **32**, **34**, **37**, 38, **39**,
    **91**, 96–97, 109, 119. *See also* crests;
    Reid, Bill
trade, 12, 16, 25, 33, 50, 67, 68, 71, 73, 75,
    80, 96, 101, 112
transportation, 12, 25, 28, 40. *See also* canoes

treaties, 106
Tsimshian, 47, 68, 70, 76

values, 41–45, 48–50, 59, 61
villages, 15, **30–31**, 31–33, 35, **94–95**, 106
reconstruction project, 116
visions, 82, 86

war, 12, 15, 41, 73, 74–77, 80
wealth, 41–42, 44, 48–50, 54, 68
weapons, 75, 76–77
websites, 123–124
whales, 19, 20–22, 47, 92
women, 15, 40, 54, 56, 58–59, 68, 70, 75,
    80, 86

# Raymond Bial

HAS PUBLISHED MORE THAN THIRTY CRITICALLY ACCLAIMED BOOKS OF PHOtographs for children and adults. His photo-essays for children include *Corn Belt Harvest, Amish Home, Frontier Home, Shaker Home, The Underground Railroad, Portrait of a Farm Family, With Needle and Thread: A Book About Quilts, Mist Over the Mountains: Appalachia and Its People, Cajun Home,* and *Where Lincoln Walked.*

He is currently immersed in writing *Lifeways,* a series of books about Native Americans. As with his other work, Bial's deep feeling for his subjects is evident in both the text and illustrations. He travels to tribal cultural centers, photographing homes, artifacts, and surroundings and learning firsthand about the national lifeways of these peoples.

A full-time library director at a small college in Champaign, Illinois, he lives with his wife and three children in nearby Urbana.